BLACK MAJORS: Baseball

Written by James Whitaker

Illustrated by Davian Chester

Hey there! Do you know about **Black Majors Baseball?**

You might know them as Negro League Baseball.

Negro League Baseball was where the best-of-the-best Black players played the game...

...before April 15, 1947.

Let's Play Ball!

These amazing baseball players faced many challenges but showed great talent and courage.

Let's step onto the field and meet these **Black Majors!**

Leroy "Satchel" Paige

Playing Position: Pitcher

Career Years: 1926-1947 (Negro Leagues), later played in Major League Baseball (MLB)

Key Statistics:
- Estimated 2,000+ strikeouts
- Numerous no-hitters
- Earned run average (ERA): Approx. 2.02 (Negro Leagues)

Strengths:
- Unmatched control and precision
- Variety of pitches, including his famous "hesitation pitch"

Claim to Fame:
- Considered one of the greatest pitchers in baseball history
- First Negro League player inducted into the Baseball Hall of Fame

Leroy "Satchel" Paige was known for his incredible pitching skills and charismatic personality. He dazzled fans with his fastballs and off-speed pitches, becoming a beloved figure in baseball. Despite racial barriers, he made his MLB debut at 42, proving his **timeless talent**.

Key Myth: The Mysterious Age
Legend has it that Satchel Paige was so ageless that even he didn't know his true birthdate! Some say he pitched well into his fifties, baffling batters with his signature "hesitation pitch" and proving that age was just a number.

Josh Gibson

Nickname: The Black Babe Ruth
Playing Position: Catcher
Career Years: 1930-1946
Key Statistics:
- Estimated 800+ home runs
- Career batting average: .359 (Negro Leagues)

Strengths:
- Powerful hitting
- Exceptional catching skills

Claim to Fame:
- Known for his incredible power at the plate
- Inducted into the Baseball Hall of Fame in 1972

Josh Gibson was a legendary **power hitter**. His home runs were the stuff of legend, with some claiming he hit the longest home runs in history. Despite never playing in the MLB, he made a lasting mark on baseball.

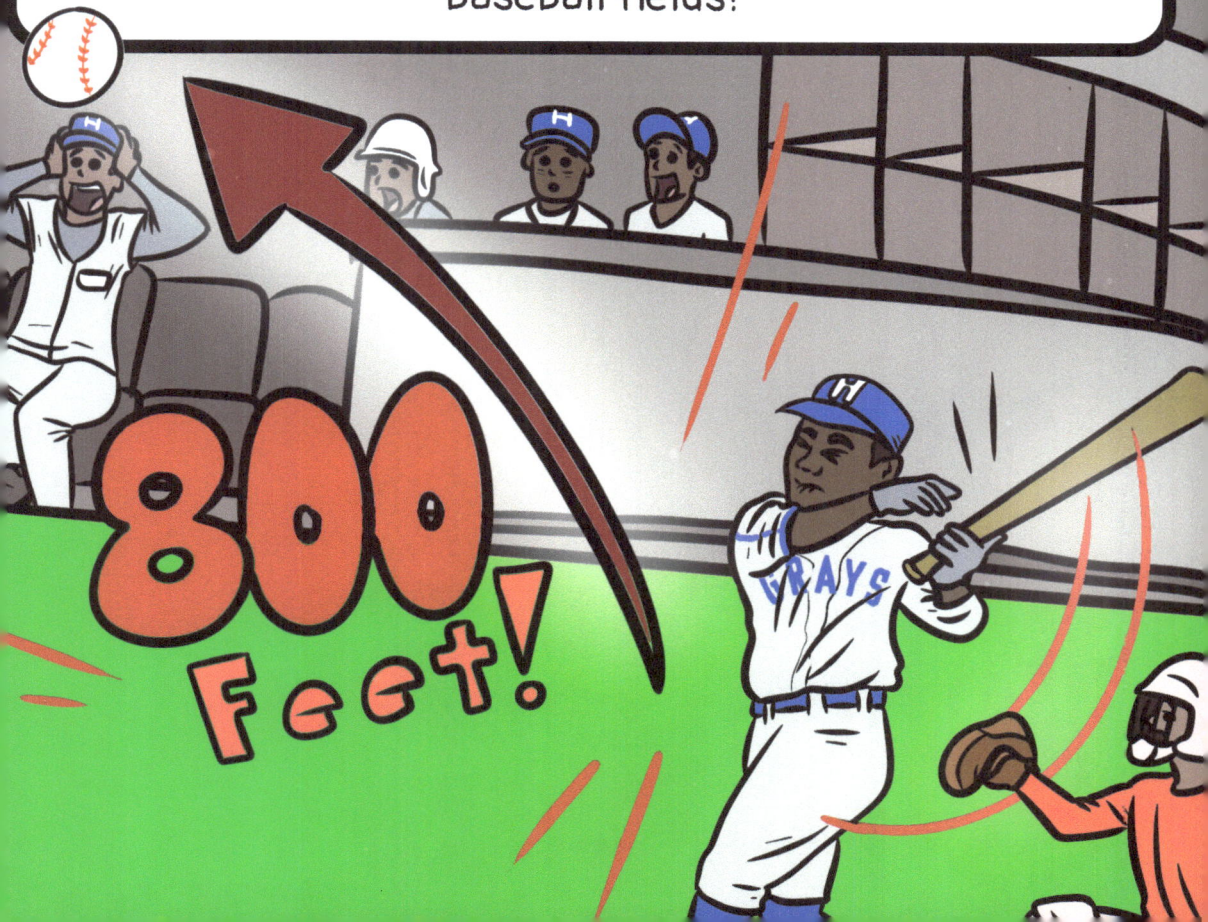

James "Cool Papa" Bell

Playing Position: Center Fielder

Career Years: 1922-1946

Key Statistics:

- Career batting average: .341 (Negro Leagues)
- Known for scoring runs due to speed and base-stealing ability

Strengths:

- Blazing speed
- Excellent baserunning and fielding

Claim to Fame:

- Regarded as one of the fastest men ever to play baseball
- Inducted into the Baseball Hall of Fame in 1974

Key Myth: Faster Than Light
It's said that Cool Papa Bell was so fast, he could turn off the light switch and be in bed before the room got dark!

Walter "Buck" Leonard

Nickname: The Black Lou Gehrig
Playing Position: First Baseman
Career Years: 1934-1950
Key Statistics:
- Career batting average: .345 (Negro Leagues)
- Numerous home runs and RBIs

Strengths:
- Consistent and powerful hitter
- Strong defensive skills at first base

Claim to Fame:
- Known for his powerful hitting and reliability
- Inducted into the Baseball Hall of Fame in 1972

Walter "Buck" Leonard was a consistent power hitter and an outstanding **first baseman**. Leonard's impressive stats and leadership qualities made him a cornerstone of the Homestead Grays, one of the best teams in the Negro Leagues.

Key Myth: The Iron Horse of the Negro Leagues
The myth goes that Buck Leonard never missed a game due to injury, showing his durability and commitment to his team!

Monford Merrill Irvin

Nickname: Monte

Playing Position: Outfielder

Career Years: 1938-1948 (Negro Leagues), later played in MLB

Key Statistics:
- Career batting average: .337 (Negro Leagues)
- Powerful hitting with numerous home runs

Strengths:
- Versatile outfielder with a strong arm
- Excellent hitter in both power and batting average

Claim to Fame:
- Excelled in both the Negro Leagues and MLB
- Inducted into the Baseball Hall of Fame in 1973

Monte Irvin was a versatile and talented outfielder known for his **strong arm** and **powerful bat**. He shined in the Negro Leagues before becoming a star in MLB, breaking barriers and proving his skill on a larger stage.

Key Myth: The All-Star in Every League
The legend of Monte Irvin states that he was an All-Star in every league he played in, from the Negro Leagues to Major League Baseball!

The stories of Satchel Paige, Josh Gibson, Cool Papa Bell, Buck Leonard, and Monte Irvin show the incredible talent of Negro League Baseball players. Despite facing many challenges, these legends left an unforgettable legacy.

Indeed, **Black Majors** were legendary and there were others!

Willie Wells
Buck O'Neil
Wilber "Bullet" Rogan
John Henry "Pop" Lloyd
Judy Johnson
Ray Dandridge
Leon Day
Martin Dihigo
Rube Foster
Oscar Charleston

Jackie Robinson
Larry Doby
Roy Campanella
Willie Mays
Hank Aaron

Who will be next?

www.ingramcontent.com/pod-product-compliance
Lightning Source LLC
Chambersburg PA
CBHW050913210326
41597CB00002B/105